Child of Clay

A traditional Venda tale

Dawn Ridgway
Illustrated by Ian Lusted

CAMBRIDGE
UNIVERSITY PRESS

There was once a woman, Dovhani, who had no children. Her husband was a rich man who owned many cattle.

One day her husband said to her, "We have no one to take care of our cattle. If only we had a son, he could take the cattle out to graze."

That night Dovhani lay awake thinking. By
morning she had an idea.

"What if I were to make a child from clay?"

As soon as the sun came up and spread its golden flush over the veld, Dovhani set off for the clay pits. There she took some of the finest clay and made the child. She stood back and smiled.

"This child must not be caught in the rain, for he is made of clay," said Dovhani. So she made him a small flute to play.

"I will always know where he is by the sound of his flute," she thought.

The next morning, Dovhani sent Mbungwa, the child of clay, out to the fields to graze the cattle.

Dovhani looked out over the fields. Great storm clouds were gathering. "These clouds will surely bring the rain," thought Dovhani. "I must call to Mbungwa and warn him that the storm is coming."

Dovhani ran to a nearby antheap. She climbed up and sang to the child of clay.

"Oh dear, oh dear, Mbungwa my child! Take care, the rain clouds are gathering. Come home, come home," she sang.

Then she heard Mbungwa's answer. The
notes of the flute came back to her on the wind.
They echoed the sound of the rain.

"A-nzhee, a-nzhee, nzhenzhele-kunzee.
A-nzhee, a-nzhee, nzhenzhele-kunzee."

Mbungwa came home, driving the cattle.
He put them safely in the kraal. Then he took
shelter from the storm in the house.

The next morning, Mbungwa again took the cattle out to graze. This time he went further from home.

In the afternoon dark clouds once again told of the coming storm. Dovhani began to fear for her child's safety and she ran to a nearby hill. She sang out her song telling Mbungwa of the coming storm.

"Oh dear, oh dear, Mbungwa my child! Take care, take care, the rain clouds are gathering. Come home, come home," she sang.

Then she heard Mbungwa's answer. The
notes of the flute came back to her on the
wind. They echoed the sound of the rain.
"*A-nzhee, a-nzhee, nzhenzhele-kunzee.*
A-nzhee, a-nzhee, nzhenzhele-kunzee."

"Take care, my child!" Dovhani told him.
"You shouldn't go so far from home."

"But Mother, the cattle need sweet grass!
And I was playing with the other children."
Then Mbungwa drove the cattle into the
kraal and took shelter in the house.

The third morning Mbungwa again took the cattle out to graze. This time he went even further from home. He took the cattle to a valley where there was plenty of sweet grass.

In the afternoon Dovhani was afraid when she saw dark clouds gathering in the distance. "Gwara! Gwara! Gwara!" The thunder crashed. The raindrops started to fall. "Guuu! Guuuuu!"

She hurried to a nearby hill. She sang her song. "Oh dear, oh dear, Mbungwa my son! Take care, take care, the rain clouds are gathering. Come home, come home!"

But this time Mbungwa had gone too far away. He could not hear his mother's voice.

She listened for the sound of his flute but all
she could hear was the sound of the rain falling.

"Plof, plof, plof . . ." Great drops of rain
began to fall.

Suddenly she saw Mbungwa driving home the cattle. But this time it was too late.

As he reached the kraal the lightning flashed, the thunder crashed and "Pwatwaa!" the rain fell. Very soon the child of clay had dissolved. He had returned to the earth he was made of.